Escape Room Success
Creating an Engaging and Profitable Real-Life Puzzle Company

Table of Contents

Chapter 1. Introduction

Welcome to an extraordinary business journey where creativity meets profitability in the most enjoyable way! Our Special Report titled "Escape Room Success: Creating an Engaging and Profitable Real-Life Puzzle Company" is a remarkable guide into the world of immersive entertainment. This report is brimming with excitement, valuable insights, successful strategies, and practical advice curated by business leaders who've turned conundrums into cash flow. With the global popularity of escape rooms ever on the rise, there's never been a better time to design a venture that amuses, challenges and rewards, all while driving significant profit! Dive into this report, and let us unravel the puzzle of creating a thriving escape room business for you, one piece at a time. Welcome, your adventure begins here!

Chapter 2. Unlocking the Concept: Understanding Escape Room Essentials

Escape rooms are a modern phenomenon that have taken the entertainment world by storm. At their very essence, escape rooms are large scale, live-action puzzles that participants must unravel in order to "escape" a themed, purpose-built room.

2.1. The Essence of an Escape Room

Simply put, an escape room is a physical challenge game in which players get to be the main characters of their own adventure story, solving a series of riddles, puzzles, and challenges within a set time limit, often one hour, to reach a defined goal. The players need to observe and use their surroundings efficiently to escape from the room or achieve the endgame.

The rooms themselves are an integral part of the attraction. Each room is meticulously designed to immerse the players in the mystery, with every piece of decor and every element of the soundtrack harnessed to create a compelling atmosphere.

2.2. The Birth and Growth of Escape Rooms

Escape rooms started to catch on in the early 2010s, with the first concepts appearing in Japan and Hungary. However, the roots of the concept can be traced even further back to the world of video games. In the 1980s and 1990s, 'point and click' video games grew in popularity, requiring players to interact with their environment by solving puzzles to move the story forward. Many believe this gaming sub-genre fed into the eventual creation of real-life escape rooms.

Today, there are more than 50,000 escape rooms around the globe and the industry itself is valued at over a billion dollars annually, and this growth trend shows no sign of stopping.

2.3. Ingredient of a Successful Escape Room

A successful escape room is more than just a room full of puzzles. It is an intricately designed, thematically consistent experience that engages and challenges its participants on multiple levels. Here are the key elements:

1. Theme: A strong, engaging theme is vital. It provides the context for the mystery and helps immerse the players in the game.

2. Puzzles: Puzzles are central to the escape room experience. They should be challenging but solvable, encouraging teamwork and varied skill sets.

3. Storyline: A compelling storyline makes the game immersive and adds emotional depth.

4. Set Design: The physical environment of the room is a crucial tool in creating a sense of reality for the players' narrative.

5. Game Flow: The sequence and structure of puzzles, as well as how clues are revealed, affect the pace and tension of the game.

6. Customer Experience: Beyond the room itself, other factors like the booking process, staff interaction, and post-game experience also contribute to the overall perception of the escape room business.

2.4. Business Perspective: Profit and Sustainability

While creativity and innovation are key to designing an engaging escape room, profitability and sustainability must always be top of mind. This involves considering factors like:

1. Revenue Streams: Ticket sales are the primary source of revenue, but consider other options such as corporate events, birthday parties, merchandising, and upselling opportunity.

2. Operating Costs: This includes rent, utilities, employee salaries, room maintenance, and marketing.

3. Investment Costs: It takes time and money to build a room and develop the puzzles and storyline.

4. Sustainability: Consider how often you'll need to change or update your rooms to keep them fresh for repeat customers.

2.5. The Audience: Who Plays and Why

Understanding your audience is another critical aspect. Escape rooms are popular with a wide demographic, from teenagers to seniors. They are used for team-building events, family outings, date nights, birthday parties, and more. Understanding the motivations of these different groups can help you tailor your rooms and your marketing strategy to their preferences.

In conclusion, creating a successful escape room business is about balancing the elements of engagement and profitability. Understanding these fundamentals is your key to find success in this innovative, rapidly growing industry. The right mix of creativity, business acumen, and a deep understanding of your audience will set you on the path to unlocking the ultimate escape room concept. Good luck and may the adventures begin!

Chapter 3. Mapping Your Market: Uncovering Potential Customer Base

Before we can dream about designing captivating puzzles and intriguing storylines, we need to first understand the audience we are building for. Recognizing your potential customer base is an integral part of constructing a successful escape room business. Developing a comprehensive understanding of your market is paramount for ensuring your business not only survives but thrives in the ever-evolving escape room industry.

3.1. Identifying Your Target Demographic

When it comes to the escape room industry, there is a broad spectrum of potential customers you could target. From enthusiasts who relish the thrill of solving complex conundrums to families, friends, and co-workers looking for interactive leisure activities, there is an abundance of possible clienteles.

You must conduct market research to obtain a well-detailed demographic profile of your potential audience. This could include their age group, profession, interests, and the reasons they seek out activities like escape rooms. Such insights will significantly influence not only your marketing strategy but also the design and theme of your escape rooms.

3.2. Understanding Consumer Behavior

Understanding the behaviors and buying habits of your customers can give you a significant edge in a competitive market. By observing current escape room businesses, attending industry conferences, and using online analytics tools, you can gain vital data that will guide your decisions.

For example, are the majority of your potential customers impulse buyers or planners? Do they tend to book their games online or prefer walk-in tickets? Do they care more about the theme/story or the difficulty level of the puzzles? Answers to these questions can shape your pricing, booking, and room design strategies.

3.3. Regional Specifics and Local Trends

Each market is unique, influenced by regional characteristics and local trends. Researching and understanding preferences on a micro-level can make a significant difference in how well your business is received by your local community.

For instance, in a city densely populated with students, rooms based around academic mysteries might resonate well. In contrast, a town known for its rich history might appreciate escape rooms featuring local folklore or historical events.

3.4. Industry Benchmarks and Competitors

Remember, you're not only competing against other escape rooms but also against all leisure activity providers in your region. Conduct a SWOT (Strengths, Weaknesses, Opportunities, Threats) analysis to understand your competitors' offerings and how you can differentiate your company.

Note down escape rooms that are consistently fully booked or have high customer ratings. What themes, pricing strategies or unique selling points make them successful? Such insights will help you shape your own business and stand out from the crowd.

3.5. Interactive Market Sizing

Based on your research and analysis, you should create an interactive market sizing model. This involves identifying your target audience, analyzing their behaviors, and then making forecasts about your potential share of the market.

Remember, market sizing isn't a one-time event. It's a dynamic process that should be reviewed and updated regularly in line with market changes, trends, and other relevant factors. An effective market sizing model can serve as a rudder directing the ship of your business toward success.

3.6. Networking

Finally, get out there and start networking. Attend local events and conferences to meet potential customers, peers, and influencers in your industry. Use these opportunities to talk about your business, gather insights, and forge valuable partnerships. Networking can not only help you build relationships but can also give you an "ear to the ground" when it comes to news, trends, and updates in the escape room industry.

By comprehensively mapping your market, you can design a business that connects with its audience, stands out amongst competitors, and adapts to shifts in market trends. The result: a profitable, sustainable escape room business that not only amuses and challenges but offers an unforgettable experience to its players. So let's unravel this puzzle and unlock the door to success, one piece at a time. You've got this, entrepreneurs!

Chapter 4. Solving the Location Puzzle: Choosing the Right Spot for Your Escape Room

Escaping the confines of a puzzle room requires attentive players, an intriguing narrative, creative puzzles, and last but not least, a strategically chosen location. A well-chosen location can be the difference between an escape room business that flourishes and one that fails. The challenge is to find a compatible site that aligns with your business objectives, budget, and customers' expectations.

4.1. Scout the Scene: Defining Your Target Market

Before you go scouting for your potential escape room locations, it's crucial to identify your target audience. Your target market can be as broad as adventure-seeking adults or as narrow as corporate groups looking for team-building exercises.

College towns, for example, offer a steady stream of young adults who are often eager to engage in this type of interactive entertainment. Metropolitan areas with dynamic business industries may host companies willing to book escape rooms for team-building activities.

To formulate a clear picture of your audience, consider conducting market research. Surveys, focus groups, and social media polling can provide valuable insights about your potential customers and their preferences.

4.2. Location, Location, Location: Choosing a Suitable Site

Once you've defined your target market, you must find an area populated by your prospective guests. Factors to consider include accessibility, visibility, local competition, and the nature of nearby businesses. It's equally important to consider cost. Leasing or buying property in a prime spot can be pricey. Commercial real estate prices vary substantially, depending on the area.

Accessibility and visibility go hand in hand. Locations near significant traffic routes, restaurants, movie theaters, shopping malls, or tourist attractions can attract a steady flow of visitors. However, a balance must be struck between visibility and cost. For instance, a downtown location might guarantee a high degree of visibility, but the lease or purchase cost may outweigh this benefit. A less conspicuous location, with effective marketing, can also draw customers.

For an escape room business, space is a substantial consideration. The selected property should accommodate multiple rooms for games, a waiting or reception area, restroom facilities, control rooms for game masters, and storage areas.

4.3. Remember to Negotiate: A Good Deal Can Go a Long Way

One of the most understated skills in finding the right location for your escape room is negotiation. Before signing a contract, it's essential to negotiate the terms of the lease or purchase, particularly for small business owners who need to regulate expenditures carefully.

Key negotiation points could include the possibility of a rent-free grace period to set up the business, escape clauses providing options for early termination, fixed rent for a specific period, or provisions for sharing some overhead costs.

4.4. Closely Study Permissions: Zoning and Legal Restrictions

Escape room operations often have to comply with zoning, safety, and other regulatory frameworks. When selecting a location, check local zoning laws to determine whether an escape room business is permitted in the selected zone.

Invest time in understanding local safety laws as well, particularly those related to fire exits, capacity limits, and accessibility requirements. Hiring real estate and legal consultants experienced in the entertainment or amusement business can be advantageous. Unforeseen regulatory non-compliance can lead to legal complexities or fines.

4.5. Sustainability and Future Expansion: Leaving Room to Grow

In the excitement of opening your first escape room, considering future expansion or sustainability may feel premature. But successful businesses often outgrow their initial premises. It's wise to give thought upfront to the potential for expansion.

Choose premises that can accommodate growth, whether that means increasing the number of escape rooms or diversifying into other immersive experiences. Ideally, you should be able to adapt the space to new trends in the escape room industry without relocating.

Likewise, choose a location that is sustainable in the long-term. Consider transport links, demographic changes, competition, and changes in leisure patterns that might impact your business.

Successfully solving the location puzzle for your escape room business requires thoughtful planning and research. It involves understanding your audience, weighing costs versus benefits, interpreting zoning laws, being adept at negotiation, and planning for the future. Taking time to get this crucial aspect right can pave the way for a prosperous and entertaining venture.

Chapter 5. Crafting Mysteries: Designing Engaging and Unique Puzzles

An escape room adventure is as good as the puzzles and challenges it presents. The thrill that players extract from decoding complex riddles, finding cleverly hidden objects, and cooperating to beat the clock is crucial to the success of your venture. Therefore, the process of crafting mysteries has to be handled with an optimal mix of creativity, practicality, and an in-depth understanding of your target audience.

5.1. Understanding Player Psychology

Understanding player psychology underlies the entire process of designing engaging and unique puzzles. This involves understanding who your players are, what they enjoy, what frustrates them, and how they behave under pressure. Concentrating on these aspects should guide the process in establishing the right balance between challenge and achievability in the puzzles you design. It's important not to make puzzles so difficult that they become off-putting, or so easy that they lack the satisfaction of achievement. You must be aware of the player's limit and make sure to construct the escape room in a way that is both challenging and exciting to them.

5.2. The Element of Surprise

The element of surprise can play a vital role in puzzle design. Unexpected twists, unexpected connections, and unexpected solutions arouse curiosity and maintain player engagement. It's also essential to maintain a balance between surprising elements and logical coherence to prevent frustration. You can achieve this balance by creating puzzles with unexpected answers that still follow a logical progression. Remember, the best puzzles are those that make the players excitedly exclaim, "Oh, now I get it!"

5.3. Integrating Technology

Technology can significantly enhance puzzle design and can be utilized in different ways to create unique, engaging challenges. RFID tags, infrared sensors, touch screens, and even voice recognition technology can introduce a new sense of interaction and immersion. But, while using technology, think about how it serves the story and the puzzles, and avoid using it just because you can. Technology should enhance the player's experience and not complicate it unnecessarily.

5.4. Consistency with Theme

The puzzles you design must also be in line with your chosen theme. If you have set your escape room in a pirate ship, for instance, modern technology-based solutions can appear out-of-place. It's also fun for the players when puzzles and solutions are based on the story. It's not only about finding a hidden key; it's about finding the pirate's hidden treasure map or decoding an ancient sea-shanty. Building puzzles that directly pertain to the narrative can significantly enhance the immersion levels of participants.

5.5. The Value of Teamwork

Design the puzzles in a way that encourages teamwork and cooperation among the participants. Escape rooms thrive on collective problem-solving, and puzzles should encourage group decision-making and interaction. At the same time, ensure that your puzzles are scalable, able to accommodate both smaller and larger groups.

5.6. Non-Linearity

Consider non-linearity in your puzzle design, as it ensures that every participant is involved in solving puzzles rather than waiting for others to complete a task. In a non-linear sequence, multiple puzzles can be solved simultaneously, allowing the team to split up and work on different tasks before reuniting for the grand finale.

5.7. Testing

Finally, but most importantly, take the time to test your puzzles thoroughly. This can be done initially by your team and later with a select group of beta testers who represent your target audience. Listen to their feedback about what puzzles were enjoyable, which were overly complex, and which didn't work at all. This feedback is invaluable for refining your puzzles and, ultimately, your escape room experience.

In conclusion, remember that the heart of every escape room is its puzzles. The thrill of solving a mystery, the satisfaction of cracking code, the joy of discovering a hidden object – these are some of the emotions that make for a successful escape room. As you design your puzzles, think about the players, infuse surprise elements, integrate technology if appropriate, ensure consistency with the room's theme, encourage teamwork, consider non-linearity, and most importantly, learn from testing. Remember, every detail contributes to creating that exhilarating, immersive, and unforgettable escape room experience that masterfully blends engagement with profit.

Chapter 6. Room Setup and Prop Sourcing: The Essential Details

Escape room design is a blend of creativity, puzzle creation, and intricate prop sourcing. Creating a cohesive room setup intimately ties into the narrative you choose. One of the key elements to constructing a successful escape room is immersive storytelling and creating an environment that sustains the illusion.

6.1. Creating an Immersive Environment

The main goal of an escape room is to provide an immersive experience. This is not merely about puzzles but creating a story, an environment that engulfs the participants and makes the reality outside the room diminish. Be it a haunted mansion, an abandoned spaceship, or a medieval castle – the objective should always be to feel like another world.

Start by penning down a narrative – a scenario that gives meaning to puzzles in your room. This narrative becomes the guide to your room setup. Just as a director uses a script to guide the production of a movie, your narrative will dictate how your escape room will come into being.

A detailed sequence of events can help in planning the room design. A well-written narrative also invokes an emotional response, capturing participants' curiosity and keeping them engaged throughout their quest.

Next, conceptualize the physical space to create the desired atmosphere. This includes the larger architectural elements - walls, ceilings and floors, down to the finer points like furniture positioning, light fixtures, and the in-room artefacts.

Every item in the room must serve a double purpose; not only should it fit your theme aesthetically, but ideally also function within the narrative.

6.2. Prop Curation and Sourcing

Props are vital components in setting the stage for your escape room; they are the elements that make your narrative come alive. While some examples of props could be locks, keys, or secret compartments, they're not limited to these. Almost anything can serve as a prop if it aligns with your narrative and can facilitate or conceal a puzzle.

When it comes to sourcing props, there are a few options available. Stores, whether physical or online, are a sure, albeit possibly expensive, way to acquire items you need. Look for antique stores, thrift shops, and online marketplaces. Props don't always need to be new; they need to fit your narrative.

A more economical way is to create props from scratch. Custom-made props often fit your narrative better and give your escape room a unique selling point. They can, however, be time-consuming to make and may require specialized skills.

Finally, a mix of bought and built items often work best. Depending on the complexity of your narrative and room design, you may want to enlist help from artists or craftspeople.

Before buying or making anything, make sure each prop has a purpose in the narrative and puzzle sequence. While a beautiful ancient vase may catch your eye, if it doesn't fit your narrative or contribute to the puzzle, it can send players on unintended tangents.

6.3. The Art of Puzzle Integration

Integrating puzzles is a two-step process: devising the puzzles and incorporating them into the room design and narrative. It is important to choose or create puzzles that align with your story, forming an integral part of the narrative arc. No puzzle should feel forced or out of place.

Consider a variety of puzzle styles like physical puzzles, mental conundrums, logic puzzles, or even musical riddles. Varying difficulties will cater to a broader audience and keep all players engaged. Just ensure all puzzles contribute to the final goal – escaping the room.

As you structure each puzzle, consider its location within the room, its role in the narrative and its complexity. Break down each puzzle into smaller parts to extend the quest duration and deepen the immersion.

Keep in mind that the ultimate objective of an escape room is fun. Always test your puzzles on different people to make sure they're challenging yet doable, and still enjoyable.

6.4. Safety Concerns and Room Design

While the goal is to create an immersive experience, it's crucial that safety is always a top priority. Escape room design requires careful consideration of safety regulations. These are not just to fulfil local laws but also ensure the well-being of your customers.

Ensure participants can exit the room immediately in case of an emergency. Secret doors or exits must not be so hidden that they aren't accessible when needed. Also, keep note of any fire safety regulations such as maximum room capacity and emergency signage.

All props should be structurally sound, particularly if they are to be manipulated as part of a puzzle. Electrical systems need to be properly installed and tested regularly.

6.5. Conclusion

A meticulously designed room setup and well-sourced props can make a world of difference in the success of your escape room. With a well-executed narrative, captivating props, complex puzzles, and a safe environment, your patrons will enjoy a truly immersive and unforgettable experience!

Chapter 7. Marketing Mastery: Attracting and Retaining Your Customers

Creating a successful escape room business calls for unique and engaging programming, but it also necessitates a compelling marketing plan to attract and retain customers. This section explores the best strategies and tactics to keep your customers interested and invested, turning them not just into repeat customers but also advocates of your brand.

7.1. Understanding Your Target Audience

The first step in creating an effective marketing strategy begins with developing a deep understanding of your target audience. Who are they, what are their interests, and how do they typically engage with escape rooms? In order to throw a wide net and reel in the rich diversity of escape room enthusiasts, you'll want to segment your audience. This could mean categorizing according to demographic factors, interests, or their relation to the idea of escape rooms (i.e., newbies, enthusiasts, experts, etc.). Make use of online tools, surveys, and market research to gather valuable data about your audience.

7.2. Craft a Unique and Compelling Value Proposition

Your value proposition is what distinguishes your escape room from others. It captures the unique aspects and benefits of your experiences and serves as the compelling reason for customers to choose you over competitors. Incorporate your understanding of your target audience and their needs in creating this proposition. For instance, if your audience appreciates brain-crunching puzzles at the expert level, your value proposition could be 'The Most Complex Real-Life Puzzle Experience'.

7.3. Developing a Multi-Channel Marketing Plan

A multi-channel marketing strategy leverages various platforms to reach potential customers. This can include social media, email marketing, search engine optimization, and traditional advertising like print, radio, and television. Each channel offers unique opportunities, and your marketing strategy should be customized for each. For example, your email newsletters could offer exclusive content, like sneak peeks into new rooms or promotions, while social media posts might include behind-the-scenes photos or user-generated content to engage the community.

7.4. Effective Use of Social Media and Video Marketing

Social media, when used strategically, can be a powerful tool for attracting customers. It provides a platform to share exciting content, engage with customers and build a community around your brand. Sharing stories around your escape rooms, spotlighting successful players, and creating immersive virtual tours can help generate buzz and interest.

Video marketing is another highly effective method to showcase the excitement and thrill of your escape rooms. Platforms like YouTube and TikTok are excellent spaces to publish a walkthrough of a new game setup or a sneak peek into puzzle-solving.

7.5. Building an Engaging Website

Think of your website as your online storefront. It should be engaging, user-friendly, and informative. Highlight customer testimonials, and include vibrant images and video walkthroughs that capture your rooms' unique experiences. Don't forget to optimize your website for SEO so that it shows up in search engine results when potential customers are searching for escape rooms or related activities in your area.

7.6. Creating a Memorable Customer Experience

The experience your customers have goes far beyond game play. From the moment they book a room until they leave your facility, every interaction is an opportunity to exceed their expectations. A seamless booking process, friendly staff, and a well-maintained & safe facility all contribute to a positive, memorable experience. Encourage customers to leave reviews and share their experiences online, and address any negative feedback promptly and professionally.

7.7. Implementing a Loyalty Program

Encourage repeat visits by implementing a loyalty program. You might offer points for every game played, with milestones for free games. Other incentives could include access to exclusive rooms or events, discounts on merchandise, or other rewards that suit your business model and audience.

7.8. Partnerships and Collaborations

Forming partnerships with other local businesses can be mutually beneficial. Consider combo deals with movie theaters, restaurants, or other recreational centers. You can also collaborate with corporations for team-building events. Such partnerships not only bring in customers, but they also help in creating a network where your business is recommended, improving overall area visibility.

By curating a tactical and creative marketing plan, grounded in a deep understanding of your audience and clear communication of your brand's unique value, you'll be well-positioned to attract and retain a growing customer base for your escape room business. Just as each room in your facility is a balance of creativity and strategy, so too is the art of marketing—it's all part of the game.

Chapter 8. Operational Guidelines: Running Tight Ships in the Chaos

Honing successful operational strategies is the cornerstone for a smooth running escape room business. Moving your business from inception to success involves numerous considerations and planning at each step. In order to figure out the puzzle for running a tight escape room business amidst chaos, we'll break down the key elements, one piece at a time.

8.1. Blueprint of The Operation

Before we dive into the specifics of running your escape room, it's critical to address the overarching roadmap of your business operations. A successful business plan doesn't merely include a financial forecast, it must also incorporate:

1. Business strategy: which includes your business model, unique selling propositions (USPs), and competitive analysis.

2. Business operations: this includes elements such as business location, hours of operation, staff recruitment and training, and an overall team structure.

3. Marketing and promotional strategies: from your website and social media strategies to communication channels with your customers.

4. Financial projections and measures for growth: this covers your basic financials, key performance indicators (KPIs), projected revenues, and plans for subsequent scaling of your business.

With this basic foundation in place, the next step is delving deeper into the key aspects of your operations.

8.2. Streamlining Your Operations

Efficiency remains paramount in an escape room business, and streamlining operations is the key. It assures smooth working procedures, reduces downtime, and increases profitability.

1. Standard Operating Procedures (SOPs): Create well-documented procedures for every task, no matter how small. This eliminates the risk of dependency on any single employee and ensures a consistent experience for customers.

2. Automation: Embrace automation tools for booking, customer communication, and feedback. This can free up your staff's time for more value-add tasks and provide a seamless customer experience.

3. Staff training programs: Routinely upskill your staff to handle diverse situations, be it technical glitches, unexpected customer behavior, or emergency situations.

8.3. Ensuring Safety and Compliance

Adhering to safety regulations and required compliance is not just a legal imperative, but an essential trust-building factor with your customers.

1. Legal Compliance: Stay abreast of all local regulatory requirements that apply to you, such as permits, public liability insurance, fire safety standards, and accessibility provisions.

2. Emergency Preparedness: Every escape room should have clearly marked emergency exits that are easily accessible, even in the midst of a game. Regular drills should be conducted to ensure preparedness.

8.4. Maintaining & Refreshing Your Rooms

Keeping your escape rooms crisp and exciting for repeat customers serves as a constant challenge and opportunity.

1. Routine Maintenance: Schedule routine checks to ensure your rooms stay top-notch. Any wear and tear, broken props, or malfunctioning of equipment should be promptly addressed.

2. Room Refreshment: On a regular basis, be it yearly or bi-annually, consider changing your room themes and puzzles. This not only attracts first-time customers but lures previous guests to revisit.

8.5. Customer Service Excellence

Exceptional customer service is the key to repeat business and strong word-of-mouth referral.

1. Staff Training: Ensure that your staff is trained in customer handling. Every customer touch-point should leave a positive impression.

2. Feedback Mechanisms: Encourage customers to leave feedback and take each review into account for continuous improvement of your escape room experience.

8.6. Financial Management

Effective financial management ensures your business remains profitable and sustainable in the long run.

1. Regular Audits: Keep close tabs on your cash flow, revenues, and expenditure to avoid unnecessary losses.

2. Diversification of revenue: Consider additional revenue channels like selling merchandise, food and drink, or partnering with local businesses for cross-promotion.

With these considered guidelines, you can navigate through the fascinating mazes of running a tight ship in the chaotic world of escape room business. Remember, the key to success in any business is an equal balance of passion, perseverance, and operational precision.

Chapter 9. Safety First: Ensuring a Safe yet Thrilling Escape Experience

Crafting a spine-tingling escape room experience rides on a delicate balance between immersive peril and actual safety. It's essential to create an environment that transports players into a captivating narrative while ensuring all elements are free from real danger. Let's dive into the integral aspects of shaping a thrilling yet secure escape room experience.

9.1. Establishing Safety Regulations

The first step in ensuring a safe yet thrilling escape room experience is to establish robust safety regulations. This includes obeying all local ordinances and fire regulations, such as ensuring secure exit pathways and installing emergency lighting. Invest in adequate insurance to cover all possible risks tied to your venture. Regular servicing of all appliances and equipment and backing this up with robust documentation is vital in pre-empting mishaps and demonstrating compliance with safety standards.

9.2. Design Layout with Safety in Mind

A well-designed escape room incorporates a thrilling narrative into an uncompromised safety layout. Design paths that allow players to move freely without any obstruction or risk of personal injury. Avoid elements in your design that may lead to accidental falls or injury, such as rugs or exposed wires. Ensure escape room props are robustly constructed and firmly secured. Make certain there's clear path to the exit, accessible at all times regardless of the puzzles' progression.

9.3. Inspecting Props and Equipment

Escape rooms involve an extensive set of props, puzzles, and electronic equipment that all pose potential risk if not regularly maintained. Regular inspections of these elements are crucial in precluding mishaps. Employ a fool-proof system for tracking each prop's state, potential tear and wear, and conduct thorough inspections periodically. This also applies to any special effects equipment used, which must undergo proper testing and monitoring regularly.

9.4. Fire Safety Measures

Fire safety is paramount in ensuring risk-free experiences for your escape room players. Each room should comply with local fire safety regulations, which typically include installing fire extinguishers at strategic positions, fitment of emergency lighting, and clearly signposted fire exits. Escape rooms often incorporate locked doors as part of their puzzles which, in a fire event, can comprise safe egress. Always ensure alternative, instantly accessible, safe exit routes are integrated into the game design.

9.5. First Aid Procedures

In the event of an accident or health crisis, you should have a well-stocked first aid kit readily accessible. Train staff in basic first aid measures and a procedure for contacting emergency medical assistance swiftly. An accessible defibrillator is an excellent addition for mitigating cardiac emergencies.

9.6. Staff Training

An essential component of safety is the training and preparedness of your escape room's staff. Staff members should be thoroughly trained in recognizing potential risks, responding to emergencies, and enforcing safety rules to customers. Regular refresher courses ensure the team is up-to-date with the latest safety practices.

9.7. Customer Briefing

Prior to beginning the escape room experience, it's essential to conduct a detailed safety briefing with the players. This can include pointing out emergency exits, a run-through of rules, and advising players of potential hazards within the room. Make it a point to cover safety elements for every special prop or puzzle used in your escape game.

9.8. Maintaining a Safe Environment

Maintenance plays a vital role in preserving a safe environment. Regular cleanliness checks, timely repairs, prop replacements, and routine inspection of structural integrity are key. Puzzles involving strenuous physical activities must be rechecked for wear and tear frequently.

Safety should be the foremost priority when crafting an intriguing escape room experience. Incorporating safety measures not only safeguards the business from avoidable lawsuits but also assures customers engaging moments with pure adrenaline, devoid of genuine hazards. This blend of excitement stirred and safety preserved delivers a thrilling yet secure escape room experience that stands out in the market.

Chapter 10. Revenue Streams: Beyond Tickets - Maximizing Your Profit

In the business of escape rooms, alongside the traditional revenue base, there are ample ways to diversify revenue streams and maximize profit. There are unconventional methods, creative pricing strategies, secondary income opportunities, and partnerships that can contribute significantly to your bottom line.

10.1. Leveraging Creative Pricing Strategies

Creative pricing strategies consist of much more than prices directly related to the escape room experience. You should consider membership schemes, off-peak pricing, and bundle offers.

Memberships: This idea revolves around turning your customers into dedicated members who have access to exclusive benefits. This could be an annual or monthly pass that offers discounted rates per game or unlimited access within a certain period.

For example, if a game ordinarily costs $25, your monthly membership fee might be $75, giving members access to unlimited games within that month. If a member was to play four games within that month, they'd be saving $25. This idea can easily attract frequent players and provide consistent income.

Off-Peak Pricing: During quiet hours or quiet days of the week, introduce reduced prices to encourage more bookings. For instance, offer a 20% discount during weekdays or mornings when fewer people seek the thrill of an escape room.

Bundle Offers: Package deals, such as combining several games at a discounted price or pairing a game with food and drink, can offer customers an all-round experience and additional value, while also maximizing revenue for your business.

10.2. Incorporating Secondary Income Opportunities

Profit doesn't just roll in from the game tickets, there are many secondary income streams that you might want to consider.

Merchandise: Branding is an essential tool for any business. Escape rooms provide an opportunity to create a range of merchandise related to the theme of the room or the brand itself. T-shirts, mugs, caps, key chains, even custom puzzles can be sold as souvenirs or memorabilia.

Beverages and Snacks: Offering refreshments, particularly for larger groups, birthday parties, or corporate events, can be an additional income stream. You can either choose to provide these on site or collaborate with local restaurants or catering services for a portion of the profits.

Photos: Offer customers the option to purchase high-quality pictures taken during their escape experience. Professional photos are a great keepsake that can generate additional revenue.

10.3. Establishing Profitable Partnerships

Forming strategic partnerships can greatly benefit an escape room business by providing another revenue stream, enhancing visibility, and offering an enriched customer experience.

Event Management Companies: Collaboration with event management teams for corporate events, team-building exercises, birthday parties, and more can be lucrative. Offer them a commission for every booking they funnel your site's way.

Local Businesses: Work with restaurants, hotels, or bars to offer comprehensive entertainment packages. For example, customers get an escape room experience followed by dinner at a discounted price.

Theme-based Collaborations: Collaborate with movie theatres, comic book stores, etc., especially when you have a theme that aligns with a specific film or comic book.

10.4. Enhancing the Customer Experience

Though not a direct source of income, providing an exceptional customer experience can lead to repeated business and higher profits.

Special Events: Host events on holidays or special occasions. This can draw in larger crowds and prompt them to spend more.

Loyalty Programs: Reward repeat customers with discounted games, merchandise, or even free games. This not only endears customers to your business but also encourages them to bring in more friends.

Corporate Offers: Provide special offers for corporations that want to use your escape room for team-building or reward days.

In conclusion, the key to maximizing profit in the escape room business goes far beyond selling game tickets. Incorporating a mixture of creative pricing strategies, secondary income opportunities, strategic partnerships, and an enhanced customer experience, will not only diversify your income streams but can also significantly increase profits. Implement and experiment with these revenue models to see how they work best for your business and market. Start small, measure performance, and constantly adapt. With the right strategies, your escape room business can truly thrive!

Chapter 11. Growth Strategies: Scaling and Expanding Your Escape Room Business

After mastering the essentials of launching your escape room venture, the true test of business acumen comes in the form of scaling and expanding. Effective growth strategies pave the way towards greater profitability, brand recognition, and customer satisfaction. Let's delve into methods of raising your business to new heights.

11.1. Understanding Your Business Dynamics

Before initiating any growth strategies, understanding the dynamics of your business is essential. The key factors to consider are your customer base, your unique selling proposition (USP), your business model, location, and current market trends. Is your customer base growing? Is your current business model viable for expansion? Does your location provide enough foot traffic? Answering these questions helps initiate an effective growth strategy tailored to your specific circumstances.

11.2. Strategies for Expansion

Once you've dissected the dynamics of your business, you can consider a variety of expansion strategies. Here are some strategies you can consider:

1. Open Additional Locations: If your current location is successful, considering additional ones might be a viable option. Make sure the demographics and competitive landscape align with your brand positioning and target audience. A well-crafted strategic plan and comprehensive market research will be invaluable in this process.

2. Franchising Your Business: This option can lead to rapid expansion with the potential for considerable profit. However, it requires standardized operations, comprehensive training programs, and thorough documentation of business processes.

3. Event Collaboration: Collaborate with local businesses for special events. For instance, you could align with a local brewery for an adults' night out or with a school during a holiday event to generate publicity and attract a diverse audience.

4. Digitizing Your Business: Take your escape room online. Digital escape rooms can expand your business far beyond your local community, opening up global possibilities.

It's important to remember that all these strategies have trade-offs and risks. The best option depends on the specifics of your business and market.

11.3. Customer Retention and Acquisition

Just as important as physical expansion are the strategies that will keep your existing customers coming back and attract new ones. You can consider the following approaches:

1. Membership and Loyalty Programs: A loyalty program can encourage repeat visits. Special deals, discounts, or free experiences for members can cultivate a faithful clientele.

2. Social Media Marketing: Active social media marketing attracts

young customers. Regular updates, contests, and engaging content will keep your brand at the forefront of their minds.

3. Partnerships with Local Businesses: Collaborating with local businesses or institutions can yield mutual benefits. Not only does it attract new customers from their clientele, but it can also strengthen your position in the community.

4. Seasonal Rooms: Seasonal themes can renew customer interest throughout the year. Capitalize on holidays or local events to create themed experiences.

11.4. Financial Aspects of Growth

Growth requires investment. Properly handled, it pays dividends in increased profits. Thorough understanding of your business finances enables you to harness growth strategies effectively.

1. ROI Analysis: Understanding the return on investment (ROI) for each different growth strategy is crucial. This helps you determine which strategy might bring the most profit relative to its cost.

2. Break-Even Analysis: Being able to predict when your investment will start generating profit helps manage the risks involved in scaling your business.

3. Financial Backing: Consider seeking backing from investors or financial institutions if your growth strategy requires substantial funding. Remember, this might involve giving up partial control of your venture or paying interest on loans.

11.5. The Human Factor in Your Growth Strategy

As your business grows, so should your team. A larger or more diverse team may be required to manage multiple locations, new offerings, or increased customer traffic.

1. Training and Development: Regular training and development sessions ensure your team can adapt to new roles and responsibilities as your business grows.

2. Retention Strategies: Happy employees are more likely to stay with your company. Employee benefits, a positive work environment, and growth opportunities can foster retention.

3. Hiring Strategies: As your business grows, you'll need to hire more staff. Be clear on the roles you need and what skills are required to fill them.

Growth is always an exciting but challenging phase. The strategies outlined above provide a comprehensive perspective on scaling and expanding your escape room business. The most important aspect, however, is to retain the essence of your business – the fun, excitement, mystery, and thrill that made your customers fall in love with your escape room in the first place. Keep this at the core of every strategy, and you're sure to experience high levels of growth and success.

www.ingramcontent.com/pod-product-compliance
Lightning Source LLC
Chambersburg PA
CBHW062312290526
45794CB00006B/2776